Granite
and Other Igneous Rocks

Chris and Helen Pellant

GARETH**STEVENS**
GS
PUBLISHING
A Member of the WRC Media Family of Companies

Please visit our Web site at: **www.garethstevens.com**
For a free color catalog describing Gareth Stevens Publishing's list of high-quality books and multimedia programs, call 1-800-542-2595 (USA) or 1-800-387-3178 (Canada). Gareth Stevens Publishing's fax: (414) 332-3567.

Library of Congress Cataloging-in-Publication Data

Pellant, Chris.
    Granite and other igneous rocks / Chris and Helen Pellant.
      — North American ed.
      p. cm. — (Guide to rocks and minerals)
    Includes bibliographical references and index.
    ISBN-13: 978-0-8368-7906-3 (lib. bdg.)
    1. Rocks, Igneous—Juvenile literature. I. Pellant, Helen. II. Title.
    QE461.P385   2007
    552'.1—dc22   2006035963

This North American edition first published in 2007 by
Gareth Stevens Publishing
A Member of the WRC Media Family of Companies
330 West Olive Street, Suite 100
Milwaukee, WI 53212 USA

This U.S. edition copyright © 2007 by Gareth Stevens, Inc.
Original edition copyright © 2005 by Miles Kelly Publishing.
First published in 2005 by Miles Kelly Publishing Ltd., Bardfield Centre
Great Bardfield, Essex, U.K., CM7 4SL

Gareth Stevens editorial direction: Mark J. Sachner
Gareth Stevens editor: Alan Wachtel
Gareth Stevens art direction: Tammy West
Gareth Stevens designer: Scott M. Krall
Gareth Stevens production: Jessica Yanke

Picture credits: All artwork courtesy of Miles Kelly Artwork Bank. Photographs from the Miles Kelly Archives: Castrol, CMCD, CORBIS, Corel, DigitalSTOCK, digitalvision, Flat Earth, Hemera, ILN, John Foxx, PhotoAlto, PhotoDisc, PhotoEssentials, PhotoPro, Stockbyte p. 29; Cover and title page, © Diane Laska-Swanke; All other photographs courtesy of Chris and Hellen Pellant.

Printed in Canada

1 2 3 4 5 6 7 8 9 10 10 09 08 07 06

COVER: **A piece of granite.**

Table of Contents

Words that appear in the glossary are printed in
boldface type the first time they appear in the text.

What Are Rocks and Minerals?

- Many different types of rocks and minerals exist on Earth. People use them in many ways. Rocks and minerals are also beautiful to look at.

- Minerals are solid natural substances that are made of the same material all the way through. Rocks are made of minerals. They are solid, but rocks are not the same all the way through.

- One example of a mineral is quartz. If you look at a **crystal** of quartz, you'll see that it is made of the same stuff all the way through. No matter how big the piece of quartz is, it is made of the same type of material all the way through.

- Granite is a type of rock. If you look at a piece of granite, you can see that it is made of different types of minerals. Quartz, mica, and feldspar are among the minerals in granite. Limestone and marble are two other types of rock. Both contain the mineral calcite.

- Scientists who study rocks and minerals are called **geologists**.

- Geologists place different types of rocks into groups. These groups are based on how the rocks form. **Igneous rocks** form from **molten** material that cooled deep within Earth or from molten material that erupted onto Earth's surface out of volcanoes. **Sedimentary rocks** form out of layers of tiny particles. **Metamorphic rocks** form when Earth's forces heat or squeeze rocks so much that they change into a different type of rock.

- Rocks began to form about 4 billion years ago — as soon as Earth began to cool.

- The first rocks were igneous rocks. Sedimentary rocks form from rocks that have broken down. Some of these rocks are heated and squeezed until they become metamorphic rocks. If rocks are buried deeply enough in Earth's crust, they melt.

ABOVE: Minerals can have bright colors and fine crystal shapes. The yellowish mineral ettringite forms in six-sided crystals.

RIGHT: The igneous rock gabbro is mostly made of the light-colored mineral feldspar and the dark-colored mineral pyroxene.

What Are Igneous Rocks?

- Igneous rocks are rocks that formed from molten material that started out deep within Earth. Some igneous rocks formed from molten material called **magma** that cooled deep within the Earth. Other igneous rocks formed from molten material called **lava** that erupted out of a volcano and then cooled on Earth's surface.

- Because they come from the molten stuff deep inside of Earth, geologists sometimes call igneous rocks "**primary** rocks."

- Basalt is the igneous rock that makes up more of Earth's surface than any other type of rock. It covers all of the ocean floor.

- Much of the part of Earth's crust on which the continents rest is made of the igneous rock granite.

- Different igneous rocks are made of different combinations of mineral crystals.

- Felsic rocks, or acid rocks, are igneous rocks that are made mostly of the minerals quartz, feldspar, and mica. Most acid rocks are light in color and not very heavy

LEFT: This is a close-up picture of a thin slice of granite. The rock's crystals are easy to see. The gray crystals are quartz and feldspar, and the brighter-colored crystals are mica.

LEFT: These brightly colored lumps of lava are called rainbow slag. This igneous rock occurs in southern Iceland.

- Mafic rocks, or basic rocks, are igneous rocks that are made of the minerals feldspar, olivine, and pyroxene, plus a little bit of quartz. Most basic rocks are dark colored and heavy.

- Igneous rocks that form from magma that has cooled underground have crystals that are big enough to be seen by the naked eye. These rocks are called coarse-grained.

- Igneous rocks that form from lava that has cooled on Earth's surface have small crystals that you might need a microscope to see. These rocks are called fine-grained.

- Some igneous rocks are formed from molten material that cools partly underground and partly on Earth's surface. These rocks have some large crystals and some small crystals.

Granite

- Granite is one of the best-known igneous rocks. It is colorful, and its mineral crystals are easy to see. Large pieces of polished granite are used to decorate building.

- Granite is coarse grained. Its crystals are often more than 0.2 inch (5 millimeters) across. Granite contains crystals of quartz, feldspar, and mica. Quartz is white or gray, greasy looking, and very hard. The feldspar in granite may be white or pink, and the mica in the rock may be black or silvery white.

- Granite also contains **accessory minerals** such as pyrite, tourmaline, and apatite.

- A large mass of granite that has formed deep in Earth's crust is called a batholith. The magma that makes up a batholith cools slowly, often taking many millions of years. This slow cooling allows granite to form its large crystals.

- Because granite forms deep underground, the rock above it must be worn away or moved before granite is exposed on Earth's surface. Sometimes thousands of meters of rock must be **weathered** and **eroded** before granite is exposed. In other cases, the forces that create mountains expose granite.

- Granite can be easily weathered, especially in **humid** climates. It breaks down into sand and clay.

BELOW: This pinkish mass of granite in western Scotland gets its color from the large amounts of feldspar in the rock.

Gabbro

- Gabbro is an igneous rock made mostly of feldspar and pyroxene, plus a little bit of quartz. Feldspar is light in color, and pyroxene is almost black. Together, these minerals give gabbro its speckled look.

- Gabbro forms in thick sheets when large masses of magma slowly cool. Because it cools slowly, it has large crystals that are easy to see.

- Compared to granite, gabbro is darker in color and heavier. Both its darkness and its heaviness are results of the pyroxene in gabbro.

- Most gabbro forms in Earth's crust under the basalt of the ocean floors.

- Some gabbro, however, forms on Earth's continents. Some famous masses of gabbro are in Stillwater, Montana; in Bushveldt, in South Africa; and on the Isle of Skye, in western Scotland.

LEFT: Made up of dark- and light-colored mineral crystals, gabbro has a speckled look. The main colors in gabbro are black, white, and green.

Syenite

- Syenite is a type igneous rock that forms underground when magma cools deep within Earth's crust. Because it formed this way, syenite has large crystals that can be seen with the naked eye.

- Syenite can look like granite or gabbro, because it contains some of the same minerals.

- Syenite contains the minerals feldspar and quartz. It can also contain the minerals hornblende, pyroxene, and biotite. Biotite is a dark-colored type of mica.

- Most syenite is darker-colored than granite but lighter-colored than gabbro. Some types of syenite are pink, gray, or slightly violet.

- Larvikite is a type of syenite with a blue-green color that comes from Norway. It is cut into slabs, polished, and used as a facing stone for buildings.

RIGHT: Syenite has large crystals because it formed as magma cooled slowly. The pale crystals are feldspar, and the darker patches are made of mica, pyroxene, and hornblende.

11

Pegmatite

- Pegmatite is an igneous rock that is formed deep underground from magma that has cooled very slowly. Because pegmatite's crystals have had a lot of time to grow, they are very large.

ABOVE: This intrusion of pegmatite is full of large, pink feldspar crystals. It has cut into dark-colored metamorphic rock.

- Many crystals in pegmatite are more than 1.2 inches (3 centimeters) long. In some pegmatite rocks, giant crystal more than 3.3 feet (1 meter) have been found.

- Pegmatite is often considered to be a form of granite because it contains mainly quartz, feldspar, and mica. However, types of pegmatite exist that contain the same minerals as gabbro and syenite.

- Pegmatite can occur in **sills** and **dikes**.

- Accessory minerals that occur in pegmatite include tourmaline, topaz, flourite, apatite, and cassiterite. It also can contain the radioactive minerals autunite and torbernite.

- Pegmatite can contain a wide variety of rare **elements**, including niobium, tantalum, lithium, and tungsten. Some of these elements are very valuable.

- Some pegmatite looks like it has ancient writing on it. This appearance is called graphic texture. It results from quartz and feldspar crystals merging in the rock.

FASCINATING FACT

A crystal of the mineral beryl almost 19.7 feet (6 m) long and a spodumene crystal more than 49 feet (15 m) long were found in pegmatite in South Dakota.

Diabase

- Diabase is a dark-colored igneous rock with a speckled look.

- Diabase gets its speckled look from the minerals it contains: light-colored feldspar, black pyroxene, and a small amount of light-gray quartz. These are the same minerals that make up gabbro and basalt.

- Geologists say that diabase is medium grained. Its crystals are small, but they can be seen with the naked eye. To study them, however, you need a strong magnifying glass.

- Diabase may contain olivine, a greenish or brownish mineral.

- Diabase commonly occurs in dikes and sills. It is also found in the necks of old volcanoes.

- Diabase is a dense, heavy, rock that is very hard and durable. It is used in the building of roads and railways.

LEFT: Because diabase forms from magma that has cooled relatively quickly, its crystals are small. A powerful magnifying glass is needed to see the crystals in diabase in detail.

Serpentinite

- Serpentinite is a rock made from basalt and gabbro that comes in attractive colors, such as shades of green and red.

- Geologists think that serpentinite started out as the dense, heavy gabbro rock of the lowest parts of Earth's crust and that the addition of hot seawater changed it into a new type of rock.

ABOVE: Serpentinite is common on the coast of the Lizard Peninsula, in Cornwall.

- Serpentinite is made mostly of minerals such as chrysotile and antigorite. These minerals have a slippery, soapy feel. It also contains the minerals garnet, mica, hornblende, and pyroxene.

- Serpentinite is easily cut, shaped, and polished. It is used for making **ornaments**.

- Serpentinite is found in many places, including Montana, in the United States; New Zealand; New South Wales, in Australia; and Cornwall and Shetland, in Britain.

Basalt

- Basalt makes up more of Earth's crust than any other rock. Under a thin layer of **sediment**, it covers the ocean floor.

- Basalt is a dark-colored, fine-grained rock. Its crystals can rarely be seen without a microscope.

- Basalt is made of the same minerals as gabbro and diabase: feldspar, pyroxene, and a small amount of quartz.

- Basalt lava erupts nonviolently and can flow long distances. When it erupts, basalt lava contain a lot of gas bubbles. As the rock cools, gas bubbles are trapped in the rock. These gas bubbles are called vesicles. The vesicles give basalt rock a rough texture.

- Mineral deposits, including agates, form in basalt vesicles long after the rock has cooled.

- Basalt is dense and heavy because it contains minerals such as magnetite, which contain a lot of iron. The **magnetism** of this mineral has helped scientists understand how Earth's **plates** have moved.

- Rocks from the Moon that have been brought to Earth contain minerals like those in basalt.

BELOW: The flow of basalt lava can clearly be seen from the lines on the surface of this basalt mass in Iceland.

Obsidian

- Obsidian is a rock that forms when lava erupts rapidly onto Earth's surface.

- The temperature on Earth's surface is thousands of degrees cooler than underground. Because of this difference, the lava becomes solid very quickly. It forms a type of natural glass.

- Rocks formed in this way — such as obsidian — have a glassy surface and no visible crystals.

- When geologists studied obsidian with microscopes and other methods, they discovered that it is related to granite in what it is made of.

- When obsidian is broken, the pieces have sharp, curved edges. They also can be shaped easily. Primitive people used obsidian for making weapons, such as arrowheads, and other tools.

- Obsidian is a well-known rock, but it is not very common. Hecla, in Iceland, and Obsidian Cliff, in Yellowstone National Park, in Wyoming, are famous for their obsidian.

FASCINATING FACT
Pitchstone is a rock that looks a lot like obsidian.
Pitchstone, however, contains more crystals than obsidian,
and its surface is more like tar than glass.

BELOW: This is a piece of snowflake obsidian. Snowflake obsidian is often cut and polished.

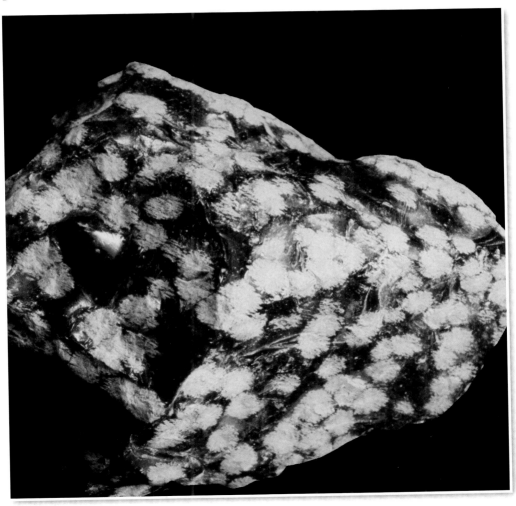

Volcanoes

- A volcano is an opening in Earth's crust out of which lava escapes.

- Some volcanoes have a single opening. These are called central volcanoes. Other volcanoes have a number of vents. These are called fissure volcanoes.

- Not all lava is the same. The type of lava that comes out of a volcano has a lot to do with how violently the volcano erupts.

- Volcanoes from which basalt lava erupts are not as violent as volcanoes that **spew** some other types of lava. Because basalt lava is hotter and less sticky than some other types of lava, it flows easily away from vents.

- The Hawaiian volcanoes, such as Mauna Loa, are made of basalt.

- The Vesuvian volcanoes, which are named after Mount Vesuvius in Italy, and the Pelean volcanoes, which are named after Mount Pelee in Martinique, erupt violently. This is because they become clogged with their sticky lava and erupt only when a great amount of pressure has built up.

FASCINATING FACT
Mauna Loa in Hawaii is the world's largest active volcano. From the seabed, it is more than 30,000 feet (9,144 m) high. The base of Mauna Loa is 70 miles (112 kilometers) in diameter.

- Earth's crust is divided into a number of plates. The plates move against one another at the places where they meet. These are the places where the crust is weakest.
- Earth's volcanoes exist along the boundaries of its plates. Many volcanoes also exist at the thinnest parts of Earth's crust.
- The floor of the Pacific Ocean is the largest of Earth' plates. The area around the Pacific is called the Ring of Fire, because so many of the world's volcanoes are located there.

RIGHT: Lava, ash, rock fragments, and gas erupt from this volcano. Its cone is built up from layers of lava and ash.

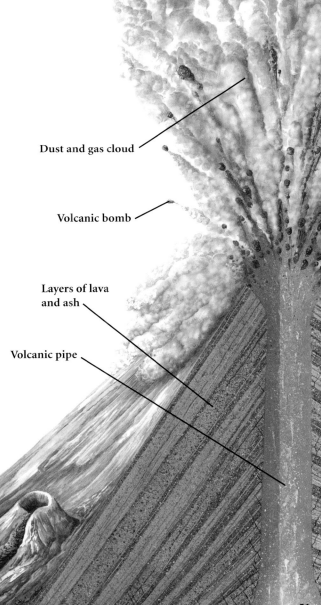

Dust and gas cloud

Volcanic bomb

Layers of lava and ash

Volcanic pipe

Batholiths

- A batholith is a very large mass of igneous rock that was originally magma. Batholiths often form deep below mountain chains.

- Batholiths may be many miles in diameter. In Britain, there is a batholith under much of Cornwall that is about 40 miles (65 km) by 25 miles (40 km). Many batholiths are even larger than this.

- Most batholiths are made of granite. Some batholiths, however, are made of other coarse-grained igneous rocks, such as syenite and gabbro.

- Even when the rock in a batholith has been formed for millions of years, heat will still rise through it from great depths. This heat is known as geothermal energy. Scientists have discovered that geothermal energy can be used to make electricity in a safe, clean way.

- Dikes and sills stretch upward from some batholiths.

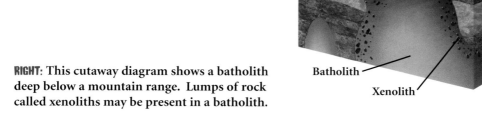

Batholith

Xenolith

RIGHT: This cutaway diagram shows a batholith deep below a mountain range. Lumps of rock called xenoliths may be present in a batholith.

Dikes and Sills

- Dikes and sills are masses of igneous rock that run through the layers of Earth's crust. They can be anywhere between a few feet thick to about one thousand feet thick.

- Some dikes and sills are made of igneous rocks that have cooled quickly and are fine-grained. One rock of this type is diabase.

- Dikes are vertical sheets of rock that cut through layers of rock. They form when magma rises to fill a gap in the rocks above it.

- Sills are sheets of igneous rock that run parallel to layers of rock.

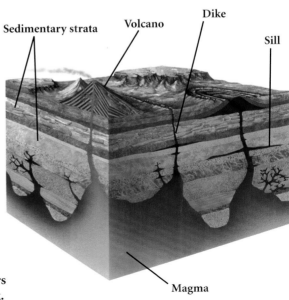

Sedimentary strata   Volcano   Dike   Sill   Magma

RIGHT: Dikes and sills are both small igneous intrusions. Dikes cut vertically through layers of rock, and sills run parallel to layers of rock.

Xenoliths

- The word *xenolith* comes from the Greek words *xenos* and *lithos.* *Xenos* means "stranger," and *lithos* means "stone."

- Many of these "stranger stones" are found around the edges of masses of igneous rock. They are pieces of nonigneous rock that break off and are surrouned by magma as the magma rises upward.

- Many xenoliths are dark, rounded, or irregularly shaped rocks set into granite or other types of igneous rock.

- Xenoliths at the edges of igneous masses are not heated much by magma, so they are not changed much from their original form.

- Xenoliths found deep within igneous rocks have been heated and squeezed. Many of them have crystals in them that are like the crystals in igneous rocks.

LEFT: The large, dark bumps in this mass of the igneous rock diorite are xenoliths.

Tuff and Bombs

- When a volcano erupts, ash and dust spew into the air. Much of this material — expecially the larger pieces — falls near the volcano.

- When this ash and dust settle on the ground and harden into rock, this rock is called tuff. Some tuff has layers like sedimentary rock.

- Ignimbrite is a type of tuff formed when volcanic ash solidifies.

- In addition to the lava that flows out of a volcano, there are also drops and lumps of lava that shoot out. These are called bombs.

- Bombs come in different shapes. Some bombs spin as they fall, which makes them long and narrow at the ends. Other bombs look like loaves of bread.

ABOVE: Thin strands called Pelee's hair form when lava is blown by the wind.

Rock Columns

- In many parts of the world, there are masses of igneous rock in which the rock has formed in almost perfect columns.

- Most of these rock columns have six sides, although they can have between three and eight sides. The columns can be **symmetrical**.

- Rock columns can be vertical or horizontal.

- Most rock columns are made of basalt. Dolerite, rhyolite, and tuff are other igneous rocks that form in columns.

- Geologists believe that rock columns probably form from cracks that develop as the rock mass cools.

LEFT: These vertical rock columns are on the Isle of Staffa, in Scotland.

Pillow Lavas

- Rounded igneous rock masses called pillow lavas form when lava flows into water.

- At certain places on the ocean floors, fresh basalt lava is always erupting. As the lava reacts with seawater and begins to cool, a glassy skin forms around some lava.

- Lava inside the skin continues to move, creating the rounded shapes of pillow lavas.

- The lava that makes up these rock formations contains pockets of gas that create the pillow lavas' texture.

- Pillow lavas occur in many parts of the world, including Britain, southeast Germany, the United States, and New Zealand.

RIGHT: These pillow lavas were formed deep in the sea over 500 million years ago.

Uses of Igneous Rocks

- Granite and similar rocks have large crystals of pink and white feldspar that give them an attractive appearance. These rocks are cut and polished and then used as facings for office buildings, banks, and other buildings.

- The dark-colored igneous rock syenite is a popular material for kitchen countertops.

- Many people buy what they think are granite countertops. These countertops are actually made of syenite or other igneous rocks.

- Durable igneous rocks such as basalt and diabase are **quarried** and crushed to various sizes. In addition to being strong, igneous rocks resist the damage of **acid rain** better than some other types of rocks.

- Crushed igneous rock is used as road ballast. A mile of new road requires more than 11,000 tons (10,000 metric tons) of crushed rock.

- Finely crushed igneous rock is used in concrete and building cement. This rock is called aggregate.

- Many gravestones are made of igneous rock.

BELOW: Granite is often used for buildings because it has an attractive surface. Tower Bridge, which runs across the Thames River in London, is partly covered by granite.

Glossary

accessory minerals: minerals that are present in a rock but are not part of the group of minerals that define the rock

acid rain: rain that contains a lot of acid as a result of environmental pollution

crystal: a piece of a transparent mineral that can have a shape with a regular arrangement of flat surfaces and angles or a rounded shape

dikes: masses of igneous rock that cut vertically through layers of rock

elements: the simplest natural substances

eroded: worn away bit by bit

geologists: scientists who study the layers of Earth and the rocks and minerals that make up Earth's crust

humid: having a lot of water in the air

igneous rocks: rocks that formed from the cooling and hardening of magma

lava: molten rock that flows from a volcano or the rock that forms when this substance cools

magma: molten material inside Earth that cools to become igneous rock

magnetism: the power to attract iron

metamorphic rocks: rocks that have been formed by the forces of heat and pressure within Earth

molten: melted

ornaments: things added for decoration

plates: the large, moving sections of Earth's crust

primary: first in time or order

quarried: dug out of an open pit

sediment: small, broken pieces of rock

sedimentary rocks: rocks that formed from the small pieces of matter deposited by water, wind, or glaciers

sills: masses of igneous rock that run parallel to layers of rock

spew: to gush out or to shoot out with great force

symmetrical: having parts that match exactly on opposite sides

weathered: worn down by the effects of wind, rain, and changes in temperature

More Information

Books

Experiments with Rocks and Minerals. True Books: Science Experiments (series). Salvatore Tocci (Children's Press)

Rock Cycles: Formation, Properties, and Erosion. Earth's Processes (series). Rebecca Harman (Heinemann)

Rocks and Minerals. Science Fair Projects (series). Kelly Milner Halls (Heinemann)

Rocks and Minerals. Science Files (series). Steve Parker (Gareth Stevens)

Rocks and Minerals. Discovery Channel School Science (series). Anna Prokos (Gareth Stevens)

Web Sites

The Dynamic Earth: Plate Tectonics and Volcanoes
www.mnh.si.edu/earth/text/4_0_0.html
From the Smithsonian Institution, this Web site features multimedia presentations on how Earth's plates move and how volcanoes work.

The Dynamic Earth: Rocks and Mining
www.mnh.si.edu/earth/text/3_0_0.html
Also from the Smithsonian Institution, this Web site features great pictures.

Rock Hounds
www.fi.edu/fellows/payton/rocks/index2.html
Information about how rocks are formed and how to collect rocks, along with quizzes and puzzles.

Index